SATs Made Simple

English

Ages 7–8

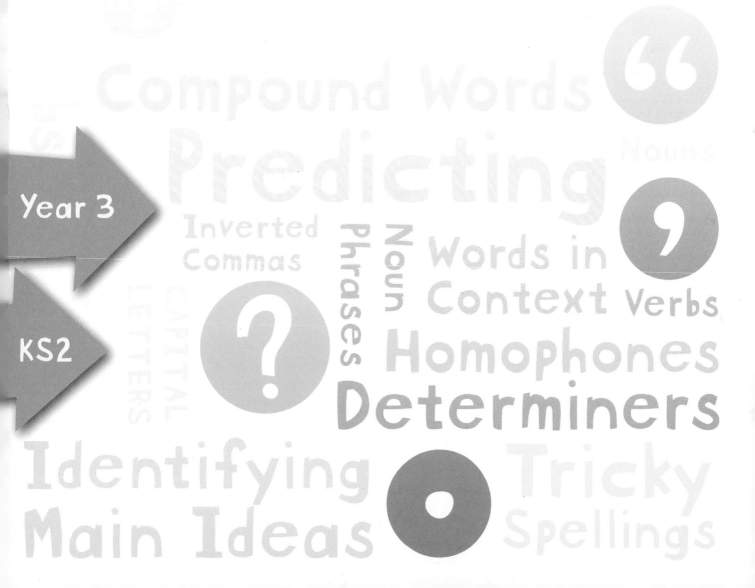

Year 3

KS2

Compound Words

Predicting

Inverted Commas

Noun Phrases

Words in Context

Verbs

Homophones

Determiners

Identifying Main Ideas

Tricky Spellings

Nouns

CAPITAL LETTERS

■SCHOLASTIC

Scholastic Education, an imprint of Scholastic Ltd Book End,
Range Road, Witney, Oxfordshire, OX29 0YD Registered office:
Westfield Road, Southam, Warwickshire CV47 0RA
www.scholastic.co.uk

© 2016, 2019 Scholastic Ltd

123456789   9012345678

A British Library Cataloguing-in-Publication Data
A catalogue record for this book is available from the
British Library.

ISBN 978-1407-18333-6
Printed and bound in India by Replika Press Pvt. Ltd.

Every effort has been made to trace copyright holders for the
works reproduced in this publication, and the publishers apologise
or any inadvertent omissions.

Author

Catherine Casey

Consultants

Lesley and Graham Fletcher

Editorial team

Rachel Morgan, Tracey Cowell, Sally Rigg, Shelley Welsh
and Rebecca Rothwell

Design team

Nicolle Thomas, Neil Salt and Oxford Designers and Illustrators

Illustration

Simon Walmesley

Contents

Spelling

Reading

How to use

National Curriculum Tests are taken by children at the end of Key Stage 2 (11 years old). Children will take tests in Grammar, Punctuation and Spelling, and Reading.

• These books are written by teachers for the National Curriculum to help children prepare for end-of-year school tests in Grammar, Punctuation and Spelling, and Reading.

• Each book is split into five sections, which match the content to be covered by the tests.

• Practising for the tests will help children feel prepared and prevent them from worrying about the unknown.

• Use the books to practise skills 'little and often'. Don't attempt to do too much in one session.

• At the back of the book is a **Planner** to enable you to record what content has been covered and to prioritise what still needs to be done.

• Year 3, 4 and 5 tests are not compulsory but SATs Made Simple will help children preparing for assessments and tests in school.

• A series of **Practice Tests** is available to help children towards the next stage of their preparations for National and school tests.

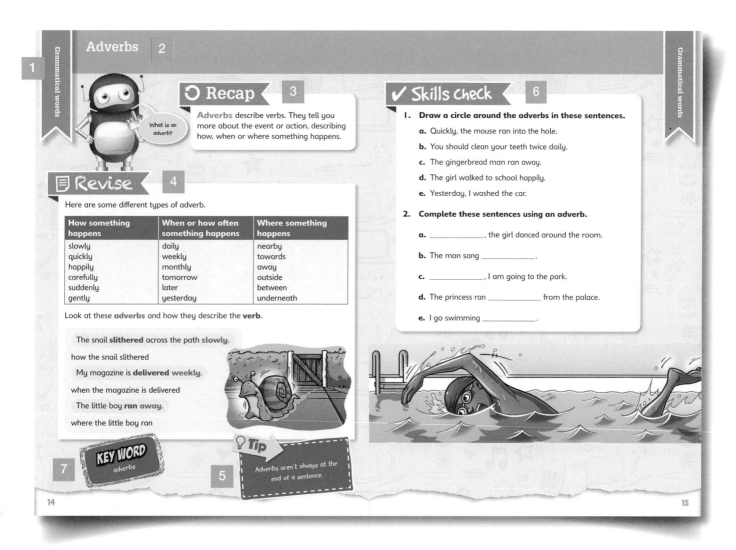

1 Chapter title

2 Subject title

3 Each page starts with a **recap** and a 'What is...' question which gives children a clear definition for the terminology used.

4 In the **revise** section there are clear teaching examples, using fun characters and clear illustrations and diagrams.

5 **Tips** are included to help show important points to remember and to give helpful strategies for remembering.

6 The **skills check** sections enable children to practise what they have learnt using National Test-style questions.

7 **Key words** that children need to know are displayed. Definitions for these words can be found in the **Glossary**.

Common nouns

↻ Recap

A **common noun** names something in general.

KEY WORDS
common nouns

📄 Revise

girl   lady   man   child   wife

these are names of people

park   school   forest   garden

these are names of places

table   book   door   cake   toys   rabbit

these are names of things

Look at these nouns.

At the **park** the little **boy** was on the **swing**.

↖ name of a place   ↖ name of a person   ↖ name of a thing

Tip

Common nouns always start with a small letter, not a capital letter.

✔ Skills check

1. Draw a circle around the nouns in these sentences.

a. The children saw an elephant at the zoo.

b. The family sat at the big table in the cafe.

c. In the staffroom, the teacher drank her coffee.

d. The footballer kicked the ball at the goal.

e. Slowly, the rabbit nibbled the carrots.

Proper nouns

What is a proper noun?

↺ Recap

A **proper noun** names a particular person, place, day of the week or month. Proper nouns always start with a capital letter.

📄 Revise

In this table, the nouns have been sorted into common and proper nouns.

Common noun	Proper noun
teacher	Mrs Green
sister	Amira
city	London

KEY WORDS

proper nouns

Look at theses nouns. Adam is the name of a person. Birmingham is the name of a place. They are both proper nouns.

Adam went to **Birmingham** on the **train**.

↖ proper noun ↗   ↖ common noun

✔ Skills Check

1. **Copy these nouns into the correct column to complete the table.**

London   Jack   bus

train   zoo   March

Thursday   cup   pencil

Common nouns	Proper nouns

Adjectives

What is an adjective?

↻ Recap

Adjectives are often called describing words. They describe features of nouns such as colour, age, shape or size.

📄 Revise

Look at the adjectives highlighted in these sentences. They give you more information about the noun.

The **old** lady got on the **red** bus.

The **slimy** frog sat on the **green** lily-pad.

My aunt's car is **rusty**.

Tip 💡

Adjectives can be used before or after a noun, to give more detail.

✔ Skills Check

1. **Draw a circle around the adjectives in these sentences.**

   a. The little girl had blue shoes.

   b. The dinosaur was huge and scary.

   c. Quickly, the tall man ran down the bumpy road.

KEY WORDS

adjectives

2. **Use an adjective to complete each sentence in this table.**

Item	Sentence
train	The boy caught the _____ train to London.
boot	The boots were _____.
rabbit	The _____ rabbit ate the lettuce.

Noun phrases

What is a noun phrase?

↻ Recap

A **noun phrase** is a group of words with a **noun** as its main word. It often contains one or more adjectives.

▤ Revise

Look at the noun phrases highlighted in these sentences.

KEY WORDS
noun phrases
nouns

noun phrase

The **enormous grey elephant** looked sad.

adjective ↗ ↖ **noun**

noun phrase

I got on the **shiny, new train**.

adjective ↗ ↖ **noun**

noun phrase

She ate the **last sandwich**.

adjective ↗ ↖ **noun**

Tip 💡
You can use more than one adjective to describe a noun.

✔ Skills Check

1. **Underline the noun phrases in these sentences.**

a. The hot, red lava flowed out of the volcano.

b. The man sat on the last seat.

c. The girl played on the new electric guitar.

d. Loudly, the cold, wild sea crashed against the rocks.

e. The old tabby cat was licking her paws.

Verbs: present and past tense

↻ Recap

What is a verb?

Verbs are doing or being words. They describe what is happening.

The **present tense** is used for events that are happening now.

What does present tense and past tense mean?

The **past tense** is used for events that have already happened.

Verbs can be in the past tense or the present tense.

📋 Revise

Look at the verb tenses highlighted in these examples.

> The squirrel **runs** up the tree quickly. (**present tense**)
>
> The postman **collected** the letters from the postbox. (**past tense**)

This table shows you more verbs in the present tense and past tense.

Present tense	Past tense
The huge dog **barks** loudly at the postman.	The huge dog **barked** loudly at the postman.
The cat **runs** up the tree quickly.	The cat **ran** up the tree quickly.
The frog **hops** into the pond.	The frog **hopped** into the pond.
I **make** a birthday card for my gran.	I **made** a birthday card for my gran.
Slowly, the tortoise **creeps** across the grass.	Slowly, the tortoise **crept** across the grass.

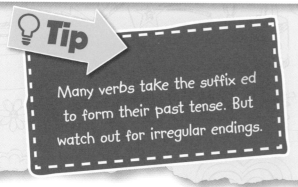

💡 Tip

Many verbs take the suffix ed to form their past tense. But watch out for irregular endings.

KEY WORDS

verbs

past tense

present tense

✔ Skills check

1. Draw a circle around the verbs in these sentences.

a. The lazy ginger cat slept on the mat.

b. Slowly, the old man walked down the road.

c. The boy ran in the playground.

d. I grated the cheese.

e. My mum made a birthday cake for the party.

f. The girl danced around the room.

Can you change past tense into present tense?

Can you change present tense into past tense?

2. Write the present tense of these verbs.

Present	Past
	walked
	posted
	slept
	made

3. Write the past tense of these verbs.

Present	Past
look	
help	
cut	
jump	

4. Complete these sentences using the correct tenses.

a. Write the present tense of the verb **washed** below.

I **washed** the car yesterday.

I _____ the car.

b. Write the past tense of the verb **eat** below.

I **eat** lunch in the garden.

I _____ lunch in the garden.

Verbs: progressive

What is the progressive form of a verb?

↻ Recap

The **progressive** or 'continuous' form of a verb describes events that were happening or are still happening over a period of time.

This verb form can be past progressive or present progressive.

KEY WORDS

progressive

📄 Revise

We use a helper verb and the main verb + **ing**. For present progressive use the helper verb am/is. For past progressive use the helper verb was/were.

Present tense	Present progressive	Past tense	Past progressive
I **dance**	I **am dancing**	I **danced**	I **was dancing**
I **talk**	I **am talking**	I **talked**	I **was talking**
He **jumps**	He **is jumping**	He **jumped**	He **was jumping**

✔ Skills Check

1. **Draw lines to match the verb form to the correct sentence.**

Verb form
Past tense
Present tense
Present progressive
Past progressive

Sentence
I cook lunch.
I am cooking lunch.
I cooked lunch.
I was cooking lunch.

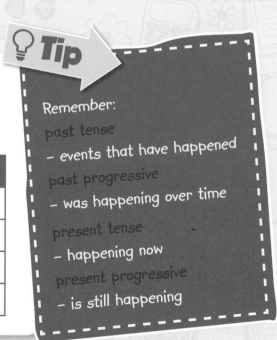

💡 Tip

Remember:

past tense
– events that have happened

past progressive
– was happening over time

present tense
– happening now

present progressive
– is still happening

Verbs: present perfect

↻ Recap

A verb tells you what is happening in a sentence.

The **present perfect tense** is used for an action that has happened at some time in the past.

📄 Revise

To make the present perfect tense you have to use have/has + a past tense verb.

> I **have listened** to that album.

> He **has been** to the shops.

Both of these show that they have happened at some time in the past.

KEY WORDS
present perfect

✔ Skills Check

1. **Change the verb to the present perfect in these sentences.**

   to sing

   a. The boy _____ in the choir.

   to see

   b. They _____ that film at the cinema.

Adverbs

What is an adverb?

Adverbs describe verbs. They tell you more about the event or action, describing how, when or where something happens.

🗒 Revise

Here are some different types of adverb.

How something happens	When or how often something happens	Where something happens
slowly	daily	nearby
quickly	weekly	towards
happily	monthly	away
carefully	tomorrow	outside
suddenly	later	between
gently	yesterday	underneath

Look at these **adverbs** and how they describe the **verb**.

The snail **slithered** across the path **slowly**.

how the snail slithered

My magazine is **delivered** **weekly**.

when the magazine is delivered

The little boy **ran** **away**.

where the little boy ran

KEY WORD

adverbs

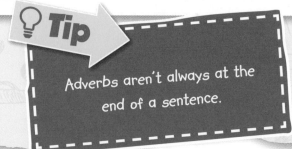

💡 Tip

Adverbs aren't always at the end of a sentence.

✔ Skills check

1. Draw a circle around the adverbs in these sentences.

a. Quickly, the mouse ran into the hole.

b. You should clean your teeth twice daily.

c. The gingerbread man ran away.

d. The girl walked to school happily.

e. Yesterday, I washed the car.

2. Complete these sentences using an adverb.

a. _____ , the girl danced around the room.

b. The man sang _____ .

c. _____ , I am going to the park.

d. The princess ran _____ from the palace.

e. I go swimming _____ .

Clauses

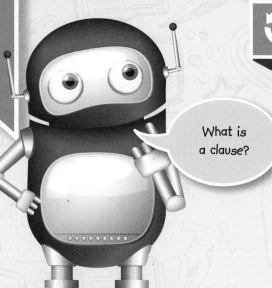

What is a clause?

↺ Recap

A **clause** is a group of words that contains a verb and tells you who or what is doing the verb. Clauses can sometimes be complete sentences.

- A **main clause** makes sense on its own.
- A **subordinate clause** does not make sense on its own.

📄 Revise

Look at the main and subordinate clauses in these examples.

I am going to the park **if I finish my homework**.

main clause   subordinate clause

It hurt when **I fell off my bike**.

subordinate clause   main clause

I like roller-skating **because it is fun**.

main clause   subordinate clause

Tip 💡

Remember that the subordinate clause needs the main clause to make sense but the main clause could be a sentence on its own.

KEY WORDS

clauses
main clause
subordinate clause

 **Skills check**

1. **Put a tick in each row to show whether the main clause or the subordinate clause is in bold.**

Sentence	Main clause	Subordinate clause
I don't like swimming **when the pool is busy**.		
I like playing football because it is fun.		
I had a new scooter for my birthday present.		
The thunder and lightning were very loud, which frightened me.		
The birds liked the new bird table **which was in the garden**.		
The car had to go to the garage **because it would not start**.		
I had a great time when we went to the park together.		

2. **Underline the main clause in each of the sentences below.**

   a. The rabbit munched on the carrots because it was hungry.

   b. I saw a beautiful rainbow in the sky when the sun shone.

   c. The teacher laughed because the story was very funny.

3. **Underline the subordinate clause in each of the sentences below.**

   a. I washed my hands after working in the garden.

   b. I was surprised when I won first prize in the competition.

   c. The old man fell asleep on the train because he was tired.

Co-ordinating conjunctions

↻ Recap

What is a co-ordinating conjunction?

Conjunctions link two words or clauses together.

Co-ordinating conjunctions link two main clauses together. They include: and but or so

📝 Revise

Look at the **co-ordinating conjunctions**. They join two main clauses together.

I went to the beach **and** I had an ice cream.

main clause   main clause

I am going horse-riding **but** I don't like horses.

main clause   main clause

Peter had pasta for lunch, **so** he was full up until snack time.

main clause   main clause

✔ Skills Check

KEY WORDS
conjunctions
co-ordinating conjunctions

1. **Circle the co-ordinating conjunctions in the sentences below.**

   a. On Saturday I went swimming and I had lunch at the cafe.

   b. It was raining yesterday but we went for a long walk.

Subordinating conjunctions

What is a subordinating conjunction?

↺ Recap

Subordinating conjunctions link a subordinate clause to a main clause. They include:

when   if   after   because   before

目 Revise

Look at the **subordinating conjunctions** highlighted in these examples.

There was a knock on the door after we returned from the shop.

main clause   subordinate clause

I hurt my hand when I fell over.

main clause   subordinate clause

✔ Skills Check

KEY WORDS
subordinating conjunctions

1. **Draw a circle around the subordinating conjunctions in the sentences below.**

   a. She laughed because the clown was funny.

   b. I washed my hands before eating lunch.

   c. The dog had a nap after she had been out for a long walk.

2. **Choose a subordinating conjunction to complete the sentences.**

   after   because   if

   a. The dentist put a filling in my tooth _____ there was a hole.

   b. I had a banana _____ my lunch.

Determiners

What is a determiner?

↻ Recap

Determiners go before a noun or noun phrase.
Examples include: the   a   an

How do I know which determiner to use?

🗐 Revise

Use these rules to help you decide which determiner to use:

- **a/an**: if you're referring to an unknown noun.
- **the**: if you're referring to a known noun.

For example:

"I think I saw **a** new **boy**," said Aaron.

↑   ↖ an unknown noun
determiner: **a**

"Which one?" asked Emma.
"**The boy** with the curly hair," confirmed Aaron.

↑   ↖ a known noun
determiner: **The**

Tip 💡

When you're using
/ : use if the noun
(or noun phrase) begins
with a consonant. "Did you
get bus into town?"
Use if the noun (or noun
phrase) begins with a vowel
(, , , ,). "I got
early bus today."

KEY WORDS
determiners

✔ Skills Check

1. **Choose the correct determiner to complete these sentences.**

   a. The girl had _____ apple for her lunch. **(an/a)**

   b. We went to the pet shop to buy _____ rabbit. **(an/a)**

   c. I dived into _____ swimming pool. **(a/an)**

   d. At the zoo I saw _____ elephant. **(an/a)**

Prepositions

What is a preposition?

↻ Recap

Prepositions link nouns to other words in the sentence.

📄 Revise

Prepositions usually tell you about place, direction or time. They include:

before   after   during   in   under   on

The prepositions have been highlighted in these examples.

> The lazy cat sat **under** the table.
> I ate all the popcorn **during** the film.
> I will go swimming **in** the morning.
> The puppy snoozed happily **on** her lap.

KEY WORDS
prepositions

✔ Skills Check

1. Draw a circle around the prepositions in these sentences.

    a. I went to bed after my sister.

    b. I woke up before the alarm clock went off.

    c. The bird sat on a branch of the tree.

    d. My knee hurt during the run.

    e. I put a packed lunch in my bag.

    f. I saw a red bike in the shop window.

    g. I hid under the bed.

Capital letters

↺ Recap

Use a capital letter to mark the beginning of a sentence.

Use a capital letter for proper nouns.

📋 Revise

Look at the capital letters in these sentences.

The children were playing football in the garden.

↑ capital letter to show the beginning of a sentence

In the garden, **A**lex was playing football.

↑ capital letter to show the beginning of a sentence   ↖ capital letter to show a proper noun (child's name)

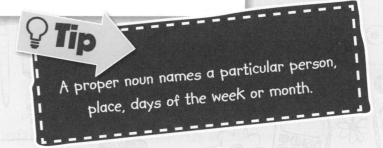

💡 **Tip**

A proper noun names a particular person, place, days of the week or month.

✔ Skills Check

1. **Rewrite these sentences with the capital letters in the correct places.**

    a. the children played in the paddling pool.

    _____

    b. on tuesday sofia went shopping.

    _____

    c. quickly, sam tidied his bedroom.

    _____

Sentence types

What is a sentence and what are the sentence types?

↺ Recap

A sentence is a group of words which make senses and contains a main clause.

There are four sentence types. Each is punctuated differently.

- Statement: a fact which ends with a full stop.
- Question: asks a question and ends with a question mark.
- Command: tells someone to do something.
- Exclamation: expresses excitement, emotion or surprise and ends with an exclamation mark.

Revise

The table below shows the different types of sentence.

Type of sentence	Example
Statement	I don't like peas.
Question	Do you like peas?
Command	Eat your peas!
Exclamation	What a lot of peas!

✔ Skills check

I. Draw a line to match each sentence to the sentence type.

Take the dog for a walk!   Exclamation

What a mess the dog made!   Statement

I took the dog for a walk.   Question

Did you walk the dog?   Command

Full stops, question marks and exclamation marks

↺ Recap

When do you use a full stop, question mark or exclamation mark?

Full stops, question marks and exclamation marks are punctuation marks that mark the end of sentences.

Full stops mark the end of statements or commands.

Question marks show the end of questions.

Exclamation marks can be used to show strong feelings. They can also be used to indicate that someone is shouting or that something is very loud.

- **.** full stop
- **?** question mark
- **!** exclamation mark

📄 Revise

Here are some examples showing when each punctuation mark might be used.

Sentence	Type of sentence	Punctuation mark
Your room is very messy.	Statement	.
Have you tidied your room?	Question	?
What a mess!	Exclamation	!
Tidy your room!	Command	!

KEY WORDS

full stops
question marks
exclamation marks

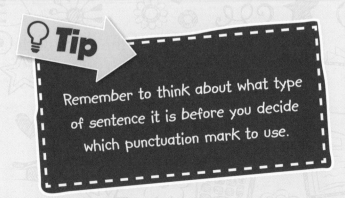

💡 **Tip**

Remember to think about what type of sentence it is before you decide which punctuation mark to use.

✔ Skills Check

1. **Complete these sentences with the correct punctuation mark.**

   Can I have a drink ☐   Get me a drink ☐

   I am thirsty ☐   What a great drink ☐

2. **In the passage below, some of the punctuation is missing. Add the correct punctuation mark in each of the yellow spaces.**

   "What a mess ☐ " shouted Adam's mum as she came into the kitchen. Flour was scattered over the table and broken eggs lay on the floor ☐ The sink was full of dirty bowls and spoons. Cake mixture dripped down the side of the cupboards.

   "I'm sorry," Adam said. "I was making a cake for your birthday ☐ "

   Adam's mum smiled. "Thank you," she said. "Now can you help me tidy up ☐ "

3. **Look at these sentences.**

   a. Tick the sentence that is punctuated correctly.

   Please can I go swimming! ☐

   Please can I go swimming? ☐

   Please can I go swimming. ☐

   b. Explain why it is correct.

   _____

Apostrophes for contraction

↺ Recap

What is an apostrophe?

An **apostrophe** is a punctuation mark: '

Apostrophes for **contraction** to show the place of a missing letter or letters, for example **I'm** for **I am**.

KEY WORDS
apostrophes
contraction

📋 Revise

Look at some examples of apostrophes used for contraction.
Can you see how the apostrophe goes where the missing letters are?
Notice that sometimes more than one letter is missed out.

Words in full	Contraction	Words in full	Contraction
do n**ot**	**don't**	I **have**	**I've**
have n**ot**	**haven't**	I **am**	**I'm**
can**not**	**can't**	you **are**	**you're**
she **will**	**she'll**		

✔ Skills Check

1. **Rewrite these words as contractions using an apostrophe. The first one has been done for you.**

Words	Contraction
I am	I'm
cannot	
do not	
you are	

2. **Rewrite these contractions using the full words.**

Words	Contraction
	I've
	I'll
	haven't

Apostrophes for possession

What is an apostrophe for possession?

Recap

Apostrophes can also be used to show **possession**, who or what something belongs to. We use an apostrophe and s.

Revise

Look at some examples of apostrophes used to show possession.

KEY WORDS

possession

I borrowed **Isaac's pen** to write a postcard.

↑

the apostrophe shows that the pen belongs to Isaac

The teacher found **Grace's hat** on the floor.

↑

the apostrophe shows that the hat belongs to Grace

The doctor looked at the **man's toe**.

↑

the apostrophe shows that the toe belongs to the man

✔ Skills Check

1. Who do the items belong to in these sentences?

a. The lifeguard found Aryan's swimming goggles in the pool.

Who do the swimming goggles belong to? _____

b. The nurse bandaged Jessica's knee.

Who does the knee belong to? _____

c. The head teacher handed out the children's certificates.

Who do the certificates belong to? _____

Inverted commas

What are inverted commas?

↻ Recap

Inverted commas are punctuation marks that show **direct speech**: " "

Direct speech is what is actually spoken by someone. Sometimes inverted commas are called speech marks.

📄 Revise

Inverted commas go at the beginning and end of direct speech. They enclose the spoken words.

I want an ice cream now.

"I want an ice cream now," demanded Emily.

Do you like carrots?

"Do you like carrots?" asked the chef.

Tidy your room!

"Tidy your room!" commanded Mum.

I don't want to go shopping.

"I don't want to go shopping," cried the boy.

💡 Tip

The inverted commas go around the punctuation too. For example, if someone is asking a question the inverted commas go after the question mark.
"Please may I have a drink?"

KEY WORDS
inverted commas
direct speech

✔ Skills Check

1. **Write the direct speech as a sentence using inverted commas. The first one has been done for you.**

Direct speech	Sentence using inverted commas
What time is lunch?	"What time is lunch?" asked the boy.
Stop!	_____ commanded the police officer.
Thank you for inviting me to your party.	_____ _____ said Layla.
My favourite lesson is maths	_____ _____ said Aahil.

2. **Add the inverted commas in the correct places.**

a. Are we nearly there yet? asked Adam.

b. We've only just left the house, Adam, said his mum.

c. Shall I read you a story? asked Adam's sister.

Commas in lists

↻ Recap

Commas can be used to separate items in a list instead of repeating the word 'and'.

🗐 Revise

Use a comma between each item in the list, except the last item when you use the word **and**.

For our picnic lunch we had **sandwiches, apples, crisps, yogurts and cake**.

I play tennis on **Saturdays, Mondays and Wednesdays**.

On the bug hunt in the woods, we found **snails, slugs, worms, beetles and ants**.

✔ Skills Check

1. **Tick the correct box to show where the missing comma should go in this sentence.**

The boy bought bread butter and honey from the shop.

KEY WORDS

commas

2. **Rewrite these sentences using commas. The first one has been done for you.**

    a. I found a crab and a fish and a shell.

    I found a crab, a fish and a shell.

    b. I saw a monkey and a lion and a tiger and an elephant.

    _____

    c. I bought a dress and a T-shirt and shoes.

    _____

Headings and subheadings

What is a heading?

↺ Recap

Headings are titles for whole pieces of text. Subheadings are titles for sections or paragraphs of text.

📋 Revise

Look at how headings are used in this text.

💡 Tip

Headings are usually in bold or bigger writing so that you can identify them easily.

Farm animals ← heading

Introduction ← subheading

There are lots of different types of farm animal, including cows, pigs, sheep, goats, chicken, ducks and goats.

Cows ← This heading tells you the paragraph is about cows.

Cows produce milk, which can be turned into cheese and yoghurt. They eat grass and hay. Baby cows are called calves. Friesian cows are black and white.

Pigs

Pigs come in lots of different colours, although the most common is pink. Pigs like to roll in mud to keep their skin cool. Baby pigs are called piglets.

Eggs

Chickens also come in different colours and they are covered in feathers. Chickens sometimes lay eggs.

✔ Skills check

1. **Read the passage 'Farm animals' above.**

   a. Draw a circle around the subheadings in the passage.

   b. How do you know they are subheadings?

   _____

   c. Read the last paragraph. Explain why Eggs is not a good heading.

   _____

Paragraphs

↻ Recap

What is a paragraph?

A paragraph is a group of sentences about the same topic. Paragraphs make text easier to read by breaking it into small sections.

📄 Revise

A new paragraph should start when the topic changes. Look at the paragraphs below.

Visiting the zoo

On Friday, Class 3 went to the zoo. The journey by coach was boring because it was such a long way. Connor got travel sick and Mrs Green had to get the sick bag very quickly.

← first paragraph: going to the zoo

When we arrived at the zoo, the zoo keeper gave us a talk about all the animals we might see. He told us where to find them, how many there were and what they liked to eat. Then, the zoo keeper gave us a map of the zoo.

← second paragraph: arriving at the zoo

First I saw the lions. They were amazing! My favourite was the huge, male lion with his big, fluffy mane. He was called Rory. He walked up and down and kept swishing his tale. There was also a baby lion. Baby lions are called cubs.

← third paragraph: lions at the zoo

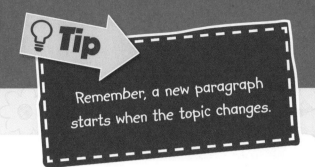
Remember, a new paragraph starts when the topic changes.

✔ Skills Check

1. Read this passage and then answer the questions below.

Next, I saw the elephant. There was only one elephant at the zoo. I thought he looked sad and lonely. He was very wrinkly and had huge, flappy ears. The elephant was very noisy and smelly. His ears were enormous. **/** Then we had our lunch at the picnic benches. Mrs Green wouldn't let us go on the swings and slide until we had eaten all our sandwiches. I didn't like my lunch because my cheese sandwiches had tomatoes in them and they were soggy. After lunch, I went to see the snakes. My little brother is scared of snakes but I think they are great! The biggest snake at the zoo was three metres long. The zoo keeper let us hold it. Its skin was all rough and scaly.

a. Draw a line like this **/** in the text to show where a new paragraph should start. One has been done for you.

b. Explain why you think the paragraph break should go there.

_____

_____

c. What is the last paragraph about?

_____

Prefixes

↺ Recap

A **prefix** is a set of letters added to the beginning of a word to changes its meaning.

For example: **un**+helpful = unhelpful

super+hero = superhero   **mis**+lead = mislead

💡 **Tip**

Prefixes change the meaning of the word.

KEY WORD

prefix

📋 Revise

Let's look at some examples of prefixes and how they work.

Prefix	Meaning	Examples
un	the opposite	unhappy, unlikely, unhelpful The shop assistant was really unhelpful.
mis	the opposite	misbehave, mislead, misspell The teacher said to the class, "Don't misbehave."
dis	the opposite	disappoint, disagree, disobey, dislike, disappear The girl was disappointed with her score in the test.
re	'again' or 'back'	redo, refresh, return, reappear, redecorate I had to redo my maths homework because it was incorrect.
super	'above'	supermarket, superhero, superman, superstar Dad went to the supermarket to buy bread, milk and apples.
anti	'against'	antiseptic, anticlockwise, antisocial The nurse cleaned my knee with an antiseptic wipe.
auto	'self' or 'own'	autobiography, autograph I was thrilled to get the footballer's autograph.

✔ Skills Check

1. **a.** Add the prefix 'dis' to change each word below. Write the new word. One has been done for you.

Word	New word
obey	disobey
appear	
agree	
like	

b. What effect does the prefix 'dis' have on these words?

_____

2. Add the prefix 'super' to change each word below. Write the new word. One has been done for you.

Word	New word
market	supermarket
man	
hero	
star	

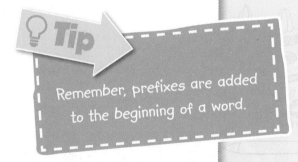

Remember, prefixes are added to the beginning of a word.

3. Draw a circle around the prefixes in these words. One has been done for you.

(mis)behave　　　autograph　　　reappear　　　anticlockwise

4. What effect would adding the prefix 'un' to the word *happy* have on this sentence?

The little boy was <u>happy</u> with his position in the football team.

_____

Suffixes

What is a suffix?

↻ Recap

A **suffix** is a word ending, or a set of letters added to the end of a word to change its meaning.

📄 Revise

Here are some examples of suffixes.

Suffix	Examples
ment	management, treatment, enjoyment
	The doctor suggested treatment for the ear infection.
ness	sadness, goodness, happiness
	My gran was filled with happiness when my baby brother was born.
ful	useful, careful, helpful
	The watering can is useful for watering the plants.
less	useless, careless, helpless
	The hose was useless because it had a hole in.

✔ Skills Check

1. **Add the suffix 'less' to change each word below. Write the new word. One has been done for you.**

Word	New word
use	useless
help	
care	
hope	

KEY WORDS

suffix

Word families

What is a word family?

↺ Recap

A **word family** is a group of words that are linked to each other by letter pattern, grammar and meaning.

📋 Revise

KEY WORDS
word families

Here is part of a word family based on the root word
teach: teacher, teaching, teaches

Look at these examples of root words and word families.

Root word	Word family
child	children, childless, childlike, childish
play	playground, playtime, playhouse, playing, played
invent	invention, inventor, inventive
solve	solution, solver, dissolve, insoluble
family	familiar, unfamiliar, families

✔ Skills Check

1. **Match these words to their word family by writing them in the correct column.**

extent   inventive   teaches   extensive

teacher   dissolve   inventor   insoluble

solver   solution   teaching   invention

invent	extend	teach	solve

Plurals

↻ Recap

Plural means 'more than one'. **Singular** means 'only one'. There are rules for spelling plural words.

Revise

For most words, to change a word from singular to plural, you add an **s** on the end.

There are other ways to change singular to plural.

For example, when the word ends in **ch**, **sh**, **ss**, **x** or **o**, you add **es**.

Singular	Plural
balloon	balloon**s**
mug	mug**s**
chocolate	chocolate**s**
book	book**s**

Singular	Plural
chur**ch**	church**es**
di**sh**	dish**es**
dre**ss**	dress**es**
fo**x**	fox**es**
tomat**o**	tomato**es**

When the word ends in **y** with a consonant before it, you add **es** and change **y** to **i**.

If the word ending in **y** has a vowel before it, add **s**.

Singular	Plural
ba**by** (b is a consonant)	ba**bies**
par**ty** (t is a consonant)	par**ties**
butter**fly** (l is a consonant)	butter**flies**
t**oy** (o is a vowel)	toy**s**
b**oy** (o is a vowel)	boy**s**

There are some irregular plurals that don't follow the rules!

Singular	Irregular plural
child	children
sheep	sheep

✔ Skills Check

1. Write the plural for each singular word below.

Singular words	Plural
toy	
car	
penny	
witch	
wish	
box	
dress	
book	
biscuit	

2. Write the singular for each plural word below.

Singular words	Plural
	brushes
	puppies
	sheep
	foxes
	drinks
	kisses
	geese
	children

💡 **Tip**

You need to learn how to spell irregular plurals – they don't follow the rules.

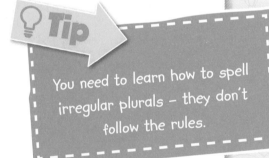

Longer vowel sounds

↻ Recap

What are longer vowel sounds?

Longer vowel sounds are produced by groups of letters that together make a single sound. They have one or more **vowels** (**a**, **e**, **i**, **o**, **u**) in them.

📋 Revise

Let's look at some examples of longer vowel sounds and how to spell them.

Vowel	Sound	Examples
a	a–e	made, came, same, bake, cake
	ay	play, hay, way, lay, day, may
e	e–e	these
	ee	green, seen, tree, three
	ea	pea, bean, sea, dream, cream, beam, seam
i	i–e	kite, bite, five, time, like
	igh	knight, night, light, sight, right, height, bright, fright
	y	cry, shy, dry
	ie	cried, lie, pie, tie
o	o–e	hope, spoke, joke, home
	oa	boat, goat, float, coat
u	u–e	tube, cube, June, tune
	oo	moon, spoon, soon, food
	ew	flew, grew, crew, new

KEY WORDS

vowel

💡 Tip

If you read a sentence out loud it will help you to identify the longer vowel sounds.

✔ Skills Check

1. **Circle the longer vowel sounds in these sentences.**

a–e ay	On Tuesday my friend is coming to play. I am going to make her a huge chocolate cake.
e–e ee ea	"I don't like these green sweets," said Danny. "They look like peas. Please can I have a different treat?"
i–e y ie igh	We flew the kite in the sky at night. It was a wonderful sight and we had a great time. My little brother is only five and he cried when we had to go home.
o–e oa	At the weekend I went on a boat. I dropped my oar into the water but luckily it could float. I also forgot my coat and was very cold by the time we got home. I hope it's warmer next time we go on the boat.
u–e oo ew	In June we planted some strawberry plants and they soon grew big with delicious strawberries on them. Growing your own food is fun.

2. **Read each sentence and look at the word in bold. Then hide the word. Have a go at spelling it, then check if you got it right.**

Sentence	Word	Spell it
The moon shone **brightly**.	**brightly**	
The bird **flew** into the nest.	**flew**	
My aunty gave us sweets as a **treat**.	**treat**	
The blue **boat** sailed across the sea.	**boat**	
On my first day at school I felt very **shy**.	**shy**	
Last night I had a bad **dream**.	**dream**	
I was very surprised when the statue **spoke**.	**spoke**	

Tricky sounds

What are tricky sounds?

↻ Recap

Tricky sounds are letters (or groups of letters) that don't sound the same as they are spelled.

📋 Revise

Here are some tricky sounds and how to spell them.

Words	Spelling	Sound
chemist, **ch**aracter, **ch**orus	**ch**	k
chef, **ch**alet, ma**ch**ine, bro**ch**ure	**ch**	sh
science, **sc**ene	**sc**	s

I went to the **ch**emist to buy some medicine.
↑
Here the **ch** makes a **k** sound.

My favourite **ch**aracter in the story was the hedgehog.
↑
Here the **ch** makes a **k** sound.

The **ch**ef cooked a delicious soup.
↑
Here the **ch** makes a **sh** sound.

We did an experiment in **sc**ience today.
↑
Here the **sc** makes a **s** sound.

✔ Skills Check

1. **Sort these words according to the sound they make. Copy them into the correct circle.**

   chorus   chef   brochure   character
   machine   chalet   chemist

k sound

sh sound

Tricky endings

What are tricky endings?

↻ Recap

Tricky endings are word endings that sound the same, or very similar, but are spelled differently.

Revise

Let's look at some examples of the tricky endings **dge**, **gue** and **que**.

Ending	Examples
dge	bri**dge**, fu**dge**, ba**dge**, e**dge**
gue	ton**gue**, lea**gue**
que	uni**que**, anti**que**

The old weak bri**dge** went over the canal.

↑

dge makes a **j** sound

That rude girl stuck her ton**gue** out at me!

↑

gue makes a **g** sound

The princess's dress was uni**que**.

↑

que makes a **k** sound

✔ Skills Check

1. **Rewrite the misspelled word in each sentence with the correct ending. The first one has been done for you.**

   a. I bit the end of my (tong). <u>tongue</u>

   b. My football team moved up the leag. _____

   c. My gran always sat in her antik chair. _____

   d. I bought some fudg on holiday. _____

43

Tricky words

↺ Recap

Tricky words are difficult to spell. They often don't follow spelling rules.

Practise spelling the tricky words on page 68.

🗐 Revise

There are lots of different ways to practise spelling tricky words.

- Practise writing them again and again.
- Try writing them in chalk outside.
- Write them in coloured icing.
- Pick six tricky words and challenge yourself to use them in a story.
- Write the tricky word again and again in a long line, but each time see if you can write the word smaller. How many times can you write the word before it is too small to see?

For example: difficult, difficult, difficult, difficult, difficult, difficult, difficult, difficult, difficult

💡 Tips

With very tricky words, make up a rhyme using each letter of the word to help you remember it. This method is called a mnemonic.

through – Tractors hurry round, over under grassy hills.

Sometimes the meaning of the word can help you remember how to spell it. For example, bicycle – bi means two or twice in Latin. A bicycle has two wheels, so this might help you remember that bicycle starts with the prefix bi.

✔ Skills Check

1. **Look at each word below. Then cover it and write it in the sentence. Check your work afterwards.**

   a. answer   Adam put his hand up to _____ the question.

   b. eight   My twin sister is _____ too.

   c. minute   We will be there in a _____.

   d. circle   The children sat in a _____.

   e. surprise   It was a _____ to win the competition.

   f. important   It is _____ to do your homework.

   g. different   I needed a _____ T-shirt to wear.

   h. difficult   The spelling test was _____.

   i. popular   Apples were the most _____ fruit.

2. **Make up mnemonics to help you remember these words.**

important		
	I	_____
	M	_____
	P	_____
	O	_____
	R	_____
	T	_____
	A	_____
	N	_____
	T	_____

surprise		
	S	_____
	U	_____
	R	_____
	P	_____
	R	_____
	I	_____
	S	_____
	E	_____

Tricky letter pairs: 'qu' and 'ph'

↻ Recap

Why are qu and ph tricky?

qu and ph can be tricky to spell as they sound like other letters.

📄 Revise

Let's look at some examples of words containing **qu** and **ph**.

Examples	Spelling	Sound
phonics, ele**ph**ant, dol**ph**in, al**ph**abet	ph	f
queen, **qu**eue, **qu**ay, **qu**een, **qu**ick	qu	kw

The **qu**een lives in London at Buckingham Palace.

At the fish and chip shop there was a huge **qu**eue.

I had to write **qu**ickly to finish the test in time.

The huge, grey ele**ph**ant looked lonely.

On our boat trip we saw dol**ph**ins swimming.

I learned the al**ph**abet song at school.

✔ Skills Check

1. **Rewrite the misspelled word in each sentence. The first one has been done for you.**

   a. The (qeen) had a beautiful crown with hundreds of jewels. _queen_

   b. I had to qeue for hours to get the tickets. _____

   c. We saw three elefants at the zoo yesterday. _____

   d. The dolfins were very friendly. _____

   e. There are 26 letters in the alfabet. _____

Compound words

↻ Recap

What are compound words?

Compound words are made up of two or more other words which together make a new word.

Revise

KEY WORDS
compound word

Let's look at some examples of compound words.

straw + berry = strawberry

tooth + paste = toothpaste

snow + flake = snowflake

pine + apple = pineapple

farm + yard = farmyard

foot + ball = football

Can you think of any more compound words?

✔ Skills Check

1. **Draw lines to join a word from each column and make compound words. Write each compound word on the lines below. One has been done for you.**

sauce	berry
pine	apple
bed	ground
snow	man
play	pan
black	room

pineapple

_____

_____

_____

_____

_____

Homophones

↻ Recap

What is a homophone?

Homophones are words that sound the same but are spelled differently and mean different things.

📄 Revise

Here are some examples of common homophones.

| knight | The **knight** rode a horse through the forest to rescue the princess. |
| night | The stars shone brightly at **night**. |

| plain | The little girl wore a **plain** dress. |
| plane | The **plane** flew through the sky. |

| sea | The boat sailed out over the **sea**. |
| see | I can **see** chocolate around your mouth. |

| grate | Can you **grate** the cheese please? |
| great | I had a **great** time at the party. |

| here | Come over **here**! |
| hear | Can you **hear** something? |

✔ Skills Check

1. **Circle the correct word. Then write it in the space provided.**

   a. The lion had a golden _____ around his head. (**main / mane**)

   b. The _____ was terrible on our holiday. (**weather / whether**)

   c. When I sat on the chair I heard it _____. (**brake / break**)

   d. We had a _____ time on our school trip. (**great / grate**)

   e. I ate the last _____ of cake. (**piece / peace**)

   f. The children put on _____ coats. (**there / their / they're**)

KEY WORD

homophones

Identifying main ideas

> What does identifying main ideas mean?

↻ Recap

Identifying main ideas means reading the text carefully and finding the key points.

🗎 Revise

Here are some of the main ideas to look for in different types of text.

Non-fiction	Fiction	
● What the text is about	● The main characters	● Key events
● Key facts	● The setting	● The conclusion

✔ Skills Check

1. **The main ideas have been highlighted in this story.**

One day, **Little Red Riding Hood's mother** asked her to take some **cakes to her grandma**, who was poorly.

Little Red Riding Hood set out into **the woods.** Suddenly, **a big bad wolf** appeared and **asked her where she was going.**

Little Red Riding Hood replied, "I'm going to visit my grandma."

The wolf licked his lips and ran ahead to Grandma's house. He hid the little old lady in a cupboard and sat in her rocking chair, **pretending to be Grandma**.

a. Who is the main character? _____

b. Where is the story set? _____

c. Who is the evil character? _____

💡 **Tip**

If there is more than one paragraph, identify a main idea from each paragraph.

Summarising main ideas

⟳ Recap

Summarising means saying briefly what the main ideas are.

🗎 Revise

The start of this story has the key points highlighted.

The lost ring

It was a hot, sunny day **at the beach**. The **twins, Carys and Gethin**, were very excited, as they put on their new wetsuits. Their mother lay the picnic rug out and set up her deckchair. Meanwhile, the **twins built a sandcastle**. Not just any sandcastle but a huge sandcastle, with a moat around it. They had just started to fill the moat with water when their mother called out that **she had lost her ring**.

Quickly, they all set about searching the beach for the pearl ring. Gethin spotted something shining in the sand. "I've found it!" he shouted, but it was just a shell. They **searched for almost an hour, finding nothing** but shimmering shells to decorate their sandcastle...

setting and main characters

main event

main event

main event

Summary of the main points:

- Twins Carys and Gethin went to the beach.
- They built a sandcastle.
- Their mum lost her ring.
- They searched for the ring but couldn't find it.

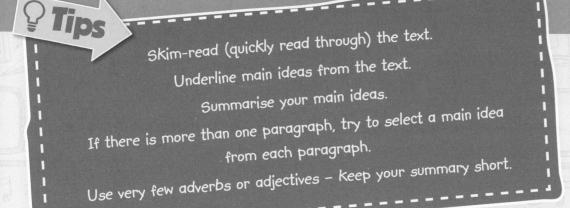

Tips

Skim-read (quickly read through) the text.

Underline main ideas from the text.

Summarise your main ideas.

If there is more than one paragraph, try to select a main idea from each paragraph.

Use very few adverbs or adjectives – keep your summary short.

Underline or highlight the main ideas to help you.

✔ Skills Check

I. Read this text and then summarise the main points.

New roller skates

Amelia had new roller skates for her birthday. She was very excited about trying them out. They were bright red with black laces.

Slowly, she wobbled down the street on them. Her arms waved around as she tried to get her balance. Her eyes were firmly fixed on her feet as she tried to get used to her new roller skates.

Amelia had not spotted the lamppost ahead.

_____

_____

_____

_____

Identifying themes and conventions

↺ Recap

Themes are ideas that go through a text. Conventions are common features that tell you what type of writing it is.

📄 Revise

Let's look at some of the features and conventions of different text types.

Text type	Examples	Conventions and features	Themes
Story	Fairy stories Traditional tales Fables Myths and legends	Characters and setting Beginning, middle and end Problem and solution Paragraphs	Good over evil Love and hate/friends and enemies Journeys or quests Wisdom and foolishness Heroism and bravery
Poem	Shape poems Limericks Ballads Nonsense poems	Verses Capital letter to start each line Exploring and playing with words	Nature and animals Feelings and friendship Everyday happenings
Recount	Diaries Newspaper articles Historical recounts	Past tense In time order Pictures/photos and captions	Personal life events Journeys and holidays News stories
Report	Information texts	Headings and paragraphs Pictures/diagrams/ photographs Bullet points	Factual subjects (history, geography, science) Accurate/reliable information
Instruction	Recipes How to make...	Equipment list Numbered points Commands (chop, mix) Conjunctions of time (first, then)	Details of how to make things (such as food, crafts, toys, furniture)

✔ Skills Check

1. **Read this text, then answer the questions below it.**

Little Red Riding Hood

Once upon a time there lived a girl called Little Red Riding Hood. One day, her mother asked her to take some cakes to her grandma, who was poorly.

Little Red Riding Hood set out into the woods. She stopped to pick some beautiful flowers. Suddenly, a big bad wolf appeared.

"Hello little girl," he said in his sweetest voice. "Where are you going today?"

Little Red Riding Hood smiled back at the big bad wolf and replied, "I'm going to visit my grandma." Then she skipped along the bumpy path.

The wolf licked his lips and ran ahead to Grandma's house. He hid the little old lady in a cupboard and sat in her rocking chair pretending to be Grandma, with her shawl wrapped around him.

When Little Red Riding Hood arrived she thought her grandma looked a bit strange.

"What big teeth you have Grandma!" she exclaimed.

"All the better to eat you with," replied the wolf.

Little Red Riding Hood screamed and screamed. The woodcutter working nearby heard the screaming and ran to rescue Little Red Riding Hood and her grandma.

a. What type of text is this? Tick **one**.

Instructions ☐   Traditional tale ☐   Poem ☐

b. Who is the hero in the story? _____

c. Which of these features are in the text? Tick **two**.

Traditional story language ☐   Bullet points ☐

Paragraphs ☐   Facts ☐

d. Give an example of typical story language used in the text.

_____

Making predictions

How do you make predictions?

Making predictions means guessing what will happen next from evidence in the text.

🗐 Revise

Let's look at an example text and use the highlighted clues below to make a prediction.

Amelia had brand new roller skates. Slowly, she **wobbled** down the street on them. Her arms waved around as she **tried to get her balance. Her eyes were firmly fixed on her feet** as she tried to get **used to her new skates**. Amelia had **not spotted the lamppost** ahead.

Now we can use these clues to make a prediction and explain the evidence.

wobbled – she was not very good at roller skating

tried to get her balance – she was unbalanced

her eyes were firmly fixed on her feet – she was not looking where she was going

not spotted the lamppost – Amelia had not seen the lamppost

What do the clues tell us?

prediction   reason

I think that Amelia will crash into the lamppost because she is not looking where she is going and she has not seen the lamppost. The text says that Amelia is not very good at roller skating (wobbled) and that her eyes were looking at her feet rather than ahead of her.

explanation of clues in the text

Highlight the clues in the text before you write your answer.

✔ Skills Check

1. Read this text, then answer the questions below.

There was a long queue to go on the bouncy castle at the school fete. Ava decided to have something to eat while she waited. She gobbled a huge piece of sticky chocolate cake before she arrived at the front of the queue.

Then Ava raced onto the bouncy castle. Excitedly, she bounced up and down as high as she could. The chocolate cake was swishing around in her tummy. She started to feel unwell. Her face turned a green colour and...

a. What do you think happens next?

_____

b. Use the clues in the text to explain your answer.

_____

_____

_____

Making inferences

⟳ Recap

How do you make inferences?

Sometimes an author doesn't tell you everything in a text. You have to use clues in the text to work out what is happening. This is called making inferences.

▤ Revise

In this example, the author does not simply write: 'Gethin does not like sun cream.' She suggests this, by describing Gethin's behaviour.

1. Read the text, then answer the questions below.

> The twins, Carys and Gethin, were so excited about their day at the beach. They loved swimming in the sea and making sandcastles. After **lots of complaints** their mother had managed to put sun cream on the twins.
>
> Gethin had **cried for ten minutes** and **turned his face away** from his mother. He complained about the **sticky feeling of the sun cream**.

why Gethin does not like sun cream

Does Gethin like sun cream? Circle yes or no.

yes / ⟨no⟩

Explain your answer.

Gethin does not like sun cream because he hates the sticky feeling of the cream on his skin and he cried for ten minutes and turned his face away.

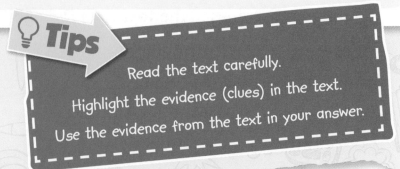

♀ Tips

Read the text carefully.

Highlight the evidence (clues) in the text.

Use the evidence from the text in your answer.

✔ Skills Check

1. **Read this text, then answer the questions. The clues have been highlighted for you.**

> It was a **hot, sunny** day at the beach in Wales. The **sun glistened** on the blue sea as the waves washed in and out. The sand was yellow and soft. The twins, Carys and Gethin, were so excited about their day at the seaside. They were wearing their new sun hats.

a. What time of year is it? Circle **one**.

summer / winter

b. Explain how you know.

_____

2. **Read this text, then answer the questions.**

> "This isn't very comfortable," complained the twins' mother, wriggling around in her deckchair. Then she found she was sitting on a shiny pearl ring! Tears of happiness rolled down her cheeks and a smile spread across her face.

a. How does the twins' mother feel when she finds the ring she had lost? Circle **one**.

happy / cross

b. Explain how you know.

_____

3. **Read this text, then answer the questions.**

> Carys was really hungry. She quickly unwrapped a sandwich from the picnic basket and took a huge bite. Suddenly she spat it back out and made a face.

a. Does Carys like the sandwich? Circle **yes** or **no**.

yes / no

b. How do you know?

_____

Language features

↻ Recap

Language features are things that writers use to make their text more interesting.

📄 Revise

Here are some important language features to look out for.

Choice of words

Look for words such as adjectives and adverbs. They make a text more interesting and help to create a descriptive picture for the reader.
For example:

> **gigantic** monster
> **old**, **rusty** car
> **Quickly**, the mouse ran into the hole.

Rhyming words

Look for words that rhyme. They make the text fun to read aloud. It can also help the text to flow and add rhythm. For example:

> **cat, sat, bat, hat**
> **crash, flash, dash**

Repeated sounds

Look for words that begin with the same letter or sound. They make the text fun to read aloud. It can also help the text to flow and add rhythm. For example:

> **G**orgeous, **g**reen, **g**rowing **g**rass

Words that describe sounds

Look for words that sound like the sounds they describe. They help to add sound to the description.

> **crash, buzz, fizz, plop, drip**

✔ Skills check

Read this poem, then answer the questions below.

Rock pools

Sandy salt water so crisp and cool,
Barnacles and shrimp all fill the pool,
Children carry plastic buckets and a net,
Their trousers are rolled but still get wet.

For shrimps and crab the children fish,
Into their net goes more than they wish.
For the biggest crab that was found,
A rock pool champion will be crowned.

In comes the tide on waves with a crash,
And the rock pools are gone, quick as a flash.

1. **Which word in the poem rhymes with fish?** _____

2. **What effect do the rhyming words have on the poem?**

   _____

   _____

3. **In comes the tide on waves with a crash,**

   a. What language feature has the poet used in this line?
   Tick **one**.

   Rhyme ☐   Repeated sounds ☐

   Words that describe sounds ☐

   b. What effect does this have?

   _____

4. **Find an example of repeated sounds in the poem.**

   _____

Words in context

What are words in context?

↻ Recap

Sometimes when you are reading, you come across a word you don't understand. You need to use the clues in the text (the context) to work out the meaning.

📄 Revise

Some words have more than one meaning and you need to work out which meaning is meant.

Word	Meaning	Alternative meaning
club	a group of people	the stick you use to play golf
light	not dark	not heavy
kid	to joke	a child or baby goat

Some words you might not know at all and you need to work out the meaning using the text.

I. The village nestled at the foot of the mountain, lying in its shadow.

What does the word nestle mean in this sentence? Tick one.

navigated ☐   sheltered ✓   disappeared ☐

Here you would choose sheltered as it talks about being at the base of a mountain and in its shadow. It's the only word that makes sense if you replaced it in the sentence.

✔ Skills Check

1. I knew I would trip over that stone on the pavement.

What does the word 'trip' mean in this sentence? Tick one.

An outing ☐   Fall over ☐   A journey ☐

2. The man was bird watching. Through his binoculars he saw a beautiful, white crane with a long beak.

a. What does the word 'crane' mean in this sentence? Tick **one**.

A vehicle that lifts objects ☐

A type of bird ☐

To look around something ☐

b. What evidence in the text tells you this?

_____

_____

3. Jonathan was very anxious about the concert. What if everyone laughed at him? What if he played the wrong notes?

a. What does 'anxious' mean in this sentence? Tick one.

worried ☐   excited ☐   pleased ☐

b. What evidence in the text tells you this?

_____

_____

Presentational features

What are presentational features?

Texts can be presented in different ways, called presentational features. They give clues about what type of text it is, highlight important parts of the text and even affect its meaning.

Revise

Here are some examples of presentational features in non-fiction texts.

Feature	Purpose
Bold writing	To highlight words and headings
Italics	To add emphasis or show that something is important
<u>Underlining</u>	To make a heading or subheading stand out, or to emphasise a word
Headings/subheading	To summarise paragraphs or sections of text
Paragraphs	To break the text into sections and make it easier to read
Pictures/photographs/diagrams	To show what something looks like, or give visual clues
• Bullet points or 1. Numbered points	To summarise the text or to order parts of it
Captions	To label pictures or photographs
Layout	To make the text easier to read and understand. • newspaper articles – in columns, large headings • instructions – numbered points

✔ Skills Check

1. Read the text, then answer the questions below.

Pitta bread pizzas ① ⑤

Delicious mouth-watering pizza ⑥

Ingredients ② ③

- 6 pitta breads
- 200g chopped tomatoes
- One crushed garlic clove
- One small onion, chopped
- 200g grated hard cheese

Method

1. Heat the oven to 180°C or gas mark 4. ④

2. First make the sauce by *slowly* frying the chopped tomatoes, garlic and onion together in a pan over a low heat for 30 minutes.

3. Once the sauce has been removed from the heat and stir.

4. Allow the sauce to cool.

5. Meanwhile, lightly toast the pitta breads.

6. Then spread a tablespoon of sauce onto each pitta bread.

7. Sprinkle the grated cheese over the pitta breads.

8. Finally, cook in the oven for approximately 15 minutes or until the cheese begins to bubble.

a. Match the features below to the numbered parts of the recipe.

Italics [4]   Heading [ ]   Subheading [ ]   Bullet points [ ]

Caption [ ]   Picture/photo [ ]

b. Draw lines to match each feature to its purpose.

Feature	Purpose
Bullet points	To summarise the text or list key points
Italics	To label paragraphs or sections
Subheadings	To show what something looks like
Photographs	To show that something is important

c. Why is the word *slowly* in italics?

_____

Retrieving and recording information

⟳ Recap

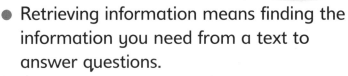

What does retrieving and recording mean?

- Retrieving information means finding the information you need from a text to answer questions.
- Recording information means writing it down.

See if you can spot the answers in the text.

🗒 Revise

The main ideas have been highlighted in this text to help answer the questions.

Mozart was a composer who lived over 250 years ago. **He was born in Austria** and wrote classical music. Mozart learned to **play the piano and violin** at an early age. He was just 11 years old when he wrote one of his famous pieces of music. **His music is still very well-known** today.

1. What country was Mozart born in? He was born in Austria.

2. Which instruments did Mozart play? He played the piano and violin.

3. Why is Mozart famous? His music is very well-known.

Now read the questions and have a go at finding the answers in the text.

✔ Skills Check

1. **Read this text, retrieve the answers you need and record your answers below.**

Famous composers

A composer is a person who writes pieces of music. Lots of people write – for example, a poet writes poems and an author writes stories or information.

Beethoven is another famous composer. Beethoven was born in Germany in 1770 (that's over 200 years ago!). He also played the piano. Beethoven wrote pieces of music about the weather and nature.

a. What does a composer do?

_____

b. Which country was Beethoven born in?

_____

c. What did Beethoven write pieces of music about?

_____

💡 Tips

- Read the text and questions carefully.
- Skim-read the text again to find the answers.
- Write each answer using examples or evidence from the text.
- Re-read your answer. Does it answer the question?

Glossary

A

adjectives are sometimes called 'describing words' because they pick out features of nouns such as size or colour. They can be used before or after a noun. The red bus.

adverbs can describe the manner, time, place or cause of something. They tell you more information about the event or action.

apostrophes:
- show the place of missing letters (**contraction**)
- show who or what something belongs to (**possession**).

C

clauses are groups of words that must contain a subject and a verb. Clauses can sometimes be complete sentences.
- A **main clause** contains a subject and verb and makes sense on its own.
- A **subordinate clause** needs the rest of the sentence to make sense. A subordinate clause includes a conjunction to link it to the main clause.

commas separate items in a list.

common nouns name something in general (boy, man).

compound words are words that are made from two smaller words.

conjunctions link two words, phrases or clauses together. There are two main types of conjunction.
- **co-ordinating conjunctions** (and, but) link two equal clauses together.
- **subordinating conjunctions** (when, because) link a subordinate clause to a main clause.

consonants are most of the letters of the alphabet except the vowel letters a, e, i, o, u.

contraction a shortened word with an apostrophe to show show the place of missing letters

co-ordinating conjunctions (and, but) link two equal clauses together.

D

determiners go before a noun (or noun phrase) and show which noun you are talking about.

direct speech is what is actually spoken by someone. The actual words spoken will be enclosed in **inverted commas**: "Please can I have a drink?"

E

exclamation marks show the end of exclamations and some commands.

F

full stops mark the end of statements.

H

homophones are words that sound the same but are spelled differently and mean different things.

I

inverted commas are punctuation used with direct speech: "Please can I have a drink?"

M

main clause contains a subject and verb and makes sense on its own.

N

nouns are sometimes called 'naming words' because they name people, places and things. A **proper** noun (Ivan, Wednesday) names something specifically and starts with a capital letter. A **common** noun (boy, man) names something in general.

noun phrases are phrases with nouns as their main word and may contain adjectives or prepositions. Enormous grey elephant/in the garden.

P

past tense verbs describe past events. Most verbs take the suffix ed to form their past tense.

perfect form of a verb usually talks about a past event and uses the verb have + another verb. **Past perfect**: He had gone to lunch. **Present perfect**: He has gone to lunch.

plural means 'more than one'.

possession a word using an apostrophe to show who or what something belongs to.

prefix is a set of letters added to the beginning of a word in order to turn it into another word.

prepositions link nouns to other words in the sentence. Prepositions usually tell you about place, direction or time.

present tense verbs describe actions that are happening now.

progressive or 'continuous' form of a verb describes events in progress.
- **present progressive:** We are singing.
- **past progressive:** We were singing.

proper nouns name something specifically and starts with a capital letter (Ivan, Wednesday).

Q

question marks show the end of questions.

R

root word is a word to which new words can be made by adding prefixes and suffixes: happy – unhappy – happiness.

S

singular means 'only one'.

subordinate clause needs the rest of the sentence to make sense. A subordinate clause includes a conjunction to link it to the main clause.

subordinating conjunctions (when, because) link a subordinate clause to a main clause.

suffix is a word ending or a set of letters added to the end of a word to turn it into another word.

syllable sounds like a beat in a word. Longer words have more than one syllable.

T

tense is **present** or **past** tense and normally shows differences of time.

V

verbs are doing or being words. They describe what is happening in a sentence. Verbs come in different tenses.

vowel sounds are made with the letters a, e, i, o, u. Y can also represent a vowel sound.

W

word families are normally related to each other by a combination of letter pattern, grammar and meaning: child – children – childish – childlike.

Word lists These are the words you need to learn to spell.

Years 3–4

accident	difficult	interest	potatoes
accidentally	disappear	island	pressure
actual	early	knowledge	probably
actually	earth	learn	promise
address	eight/eighth	length	purpose
answer	enough	library	quarter
appear	exercise	material	question
arrive	experience	medicine	recent
believe	experiment	mention	regular
bicycle	extreme	minute	reign
breath	famous	natural	remember
breathe	favourite	naughty	sentence
build	February	notice	separate
busy/business	forward/forwards	occasion	special
calendar	fruit	occasionally	straight
caught	grammar	often	strange
centre	group	opposite	strength
century	guard	ordinary	suppose
certain	guide	particular	surprise
circle	heard	peculiar	therefore
complete	heart	perhaps	though/although
consider	height	popular	thought
continue	history	position	through
decide	imagine	possess	various
describe	increase	possession	weight
different	important	possible	woman/women

Answers: Year 3

GRAMMATICAL WORDS

Page 6

1. **a.** The (children) saw an (elephant) at the (zoo).
   b. The (family) sat at the big (table) in the (cafe).
   c. In the (staffroom), the (teacher) drank her (coffee).
   d. The (footballer) kicked the (ball) at the (goal).
   e. Slowly, the (rabbit) nibbled the (carrots).

Page 7

1.

Common nouns	Proper nouns
bus	Thursday
train	Jack
zoo	London
cup	March
pencil	

Page 8

1. **a.** The (little) girl had (blue) shoes.
   b. The dinosaur was (huge) and (scary).
   c. Quickly, the (tall) man ran down the (bumpy) road.

2. Accept any suitable adjective such as:
   train – blue, shiny, new
   boots – old, muddy, dirty, brown
   rabbit – fluffy, white, small, cute

Page 9

1. **a.** The hot, red lava flowed out of the volcano.
   b. The man sat on the last seat.
   c. The girl played happily on the new electric guitar.
   d. Loudly, the cold, wild sea crashed against the rocks.
   e. The old tabby cat was licking her paws.

Page 11

1. **a.** The lazy ginger cat (slept) on the mat.
   b. Slowly, the old man (walked) down the road.
   c. The boy (ran) in the playground.
   d. I (grated) the cheese.
   e. My mum (made) a birthday cake for the party.
   f. The girl (danced) around the room.

2.

Present tense	Past tense
walk(s)	walked
post(s)	posted
sleep(s)	slept
make(s)	made

3.

Present tense	Past tense
look	**looked**
help	**helped**
cut	**cut**
jump	**jumped**

4. **a.** I **wash** the car.
   b. I **ate** lunch in the garden.

Page 12

1.

Verb form	Sentence
Past tense	I cook lunch.
Present tense	I am cooking lunch.
Present progressive	I cooked lunch.
Past progressive	I was cooking lunch.

(Past tense → I cooked lunch.; Present tense → I cook lunch.; Present progressive → I am cooking lunch.; Past progressive → I was cooking lunch.)

Page 13

1. **a.** The boy **has sung** in the choir.
   b. They **have seen** that film at the cinema.

Page 15

1. **a.** (Quickly), the mouse ran into the hole.
   b. You should clean your teeth twice (daily).
   c. The gingerbread man ran (away).
   d. The girl walked to school (happily).
   e. (Yesterday), I washed the car.

2. **a.** Accept any suitable adverb of manner or time, for example Happily, Yesterday.
   b. Accept any suitable adverb of manner or time, for example beautifully, yesterday.
   c. Accept any suitable adverb of time, place or manner that makes sense, for example Later, Tomorrow, Noisily.
   d. The princess ran away from the palace.
   e. Accept any suitable adverb of time, place or manner, for example sometimes, outside.

Page 17

1.

Sentence	Main clause	Subordinate clause
I don't like swimming **when the pool is busy.**		✓
I like playing football because it is fun.	✓	
I had a new scooter for my birthday present.	✓	
The thunder and lightning were very loud, which frightened me.	✓	
The birds liked the new bird table **which was in the garden.**		✓
The car had to go to the garage **because it would not start.**		✓
I had a great time when we went to the park together.	✓	

2. **a.** The rabbit munched on the carrots because it was hungry.
   b. I saw a beautiful rainbow in the sky when the sun shone.
   c. The teacher laughed because the story was very funny.

3. **a.** I washed my hands after working in the garden.
   b. I was surprised when I won first prize in the competition.
   c. The old man fell asleep on the train because he was tired.

1 **a.** On Saturday I went swimming (and) I had lunch at the cafe.

b. It was raining yesterday (but) we went for a long walk.

1 **a.** She laughed (because) the clown was funny.

b. I washed my hands (before) eating lunch.

c. The dog had a nap (after) she had been out for a long walk.

2 **a.** The dentist put a filling in my tooth **because** there was a hole.

b. I had a banana **after** my lunch.

1 **a.** The girl had **an** apple for her lunch.

b. We went to the pet shop to buy **a** rabbit.

c. I dived into **a** swimming pool.

d. At the zoo I saw **an** elephant.

1 **a.** I went to bed (after) my sister.

b. I woke up (before) the alarm clock went off.

c. The bird sat (on) a branch of the tree.

d. My knee hurt (during) the run.

e. I put a packed lunch (in) my bag.

f. I saw a red bike (in) the shop window.

g. I hid (under) the bed.

PUNCTUATION

1 **a. T**he children played in the paddling pool.

b. On **T**uesday **S**ofia went shopping.

c. Quickly, **S**am tidied his bedroom.

Take the dog for a walk! ——————— Exclamation

What a mess the dog made! ———— Statement

I took the dog for a walk. ———— Question

Did you walk the dog? —————— Command

1 Can I have a drink**?**
I am thirsty**.**
Get me a drink**.** or **!**
What a great drink**!**

2 "What a mess**!**" shouted Adam's mum as she came into the kitchen.

Flour was scattered over the table and broken eggs lay on the floor**.** The sink was full of dirty bowls and spoons. Cake mixture dripped down the side of the cupboards.

"I'm sorry," Adam said. "I was making a cake for your birthday**.**"

Adam's mum smiled. "Thank you," she said. "Now can you help me tidy up**?**"

3 **a.** Please can I go swimming?

b. It is a question so needs a question mark.

1

Words	Contraction
can not	**can't**
do not	**don't**
you are	**you're**

2

Words	Contraction
I have	I've
I will	I'll
have not	haven't

1 **a.** Aryan
b. Jessica
c. The children

1 <u>"Stop!"</u> commanded the police officer.

<u>"Thank you for inviting me to your party,"</u> said Layla.

<u>"My favourite lesson is maths,"</u> said Aahil.

2 **a.** "Are we nearly there yet?" asked Adam.

b. "We only just left the house Adam," said his mum.

c. "Shall I read you a story?" asked Adam's sister.

1 The boy bought bread butter and honey from the shop.

2 **b.** I saw a monkey, a lion, a tiger and an elephant.
c. I bought a dress, a T-shirt and shoes.

1 **a.** Introduction, Cows, Pigs, Eggs
b. They give titles to paragraphs of text.
c. All the other headings are the names of animals / The paragraph is about chickens / The passage is about farm animals.

1 **a.** A clear line / between 'soggy.' and 'After lunch'.

b. An explanation showing understanding that the topic has changed from lunch to snakes.

c. Snakes

VOCABULARY

1 **a.**

Word	New word
appear	**disappear**
agree	**disagree**
like	**dislike**

b. Accept any answer that suggests an understanding that the prefix 'dis' has the opposite effect.

2

Word	New word
man	**superman**
hero	**superhero**
star	**superstar**

3 (auto)graph (re)appear (anti)clockwise

4 Accept any answer that suggests adding the prefix 'un' turns the word into *unhappy*, meaning the boy was not happy with his position in the football team.

Page 36

1

Word	New word
help	**helpless**
care	**careless**
hope	**hopeless**

Page 37

1

invent	extend	teach	solve
inventor inventive invention	extent extensive	teaching teacher teaches	dissolve solution solver insoluble

SPELLING

Page 39

1

Singular words	Plural
toy	**toys**
car	**cars**
penny	**pennies**
witch	**witches**
wish	**wishes**
box	**boxes**
dress	**dresses**
book	**books**
biscuit	**biscuits**

2

Singular words	Plural
brush	brushes
puppy	puppies
sheep	sheep
fox	foxes
drink	drinks
kiss	kisses
goose	geese
child	children

Page 41

1

a–e ay	On Tuesday my friend is coming to play. I am going to make her a huge chocolate cake.
e–e ee ea	"I don't like these green sweets" said Danny. "They look like peas. Please can I have a different treat?"
i–e y ie igh	We flew the kite in the sky at night. It was a wonderful sight and we had a great time. My little brother is only five and he cried when we had to go home.
o–e oa	At the weekend I went on a boat. I dropped my oar into the water but luckily it could float. I also forgot my coat and was very cold by the time we got home. I hope it's warmer next time we go on the boat.
u–e oo ew	In June we planted some strawberry plants and they soon grew big with delicious strawberries on them. Growing your own food is fun.

Page 42

1 k sound: chorus, character, chemist
sh sound: brochure, machine, chef, chalet

Page 43

1 **b.** league
c. antique
d. fudge

Page 46

1 **b.** queue
c. elephants
d. dolphins
e. alphabet

Page 47

1 saucepan, bedroom, snowman, playground, blackberry

Page 48

1 **a.** mane **b.** weather **c.** break **d.** great **e.** piece
f. their

READING

Page 49

1 **a.** Little Red Riding Hood (or the big bad wolf)
b. In the woods and Grandma's house
c. The big bad wolf

Page 51

1 • Amelia has new roller skates.
• She tries them out.
• She is unsteady on them.

Page 53

1 **a.** Traditional tale
b. The woodcutter
c. Traditional story language / Paragraphs
d. Once upon a time

Page 55

1 **a.** Any answer that suggests Ava is sick (all over the bouncy castle).
b. Answers must refer to evidence in the text. For example, the text says:
• she gobbled a huge piece of cake just before she started jumping up and down/the chocolate cake was swishing around in her tummy, which could make you feel sick
• she felt unwell/her face turned green, which is probably a sign of feeling sick.

Page 57

1 **a.** summer
b. It's hot and sunny.

2 **a.** happy
b. She is smiling/tears of happiness.

3 **a.** no
b. She spits it out/makes a face

Page 59

1 wish

2 They help the text to flow/they create a rhythm.

3 **a.** Onomatopoeia
b. It helps us to hear the sound of the waves.

4 **s**andy **s**alt (water)

1   Fall over

2   **a.** A type of bird
     b. The context is bird watching and the writer describes the beak.

3   **a.** worried
     b. He is worried people might laugh at him or play the wrong notes.

1   **a.** 1. Heading
       2. Subheading
       3. Bullet points
       4. Italics
       5. Picture/photo
       6. Caption

     b. Bullet points ——————— To summarise the text or list key points

       Italics   To label paragraphs or sections

       Subheadings   To show what something looks like

       Photographs   To show that something is important

     c. To emphasise the word *slowly* is important / To show it is important to fry the ingredients slowly

1   **a.** A composer writes pieces of music.
     b. He was born in Germany.
     c. He wrote music about the weather and nature.